The Ongoing Struggle

Volume 2

FREEDOM IN A CAGE

Brenda S. Jackson, Ph.D.

Detroit, Michigan, USA

Freedom in a Cage
Copyright © 2013 Brenda S. Jackson, Ph.D.

All scripture quotations, unless otherwise indicated, taken from the HOLY BIBLE, NEW INTERNATIONAL VERSION®. NIV®. Copyright© 1973, 1978, 1984 by International Bible Society. Used by permission of Zondervan. All rights reserved.

Scripture quotations marked (KJV) are taken from the HOLY BIBLE, KING JAMES VERSION (Authorized).

All poetry submissions herein are © 2000 – 2012 Brenda S. Jackson

All rights reserved. No part of this publication may be reproduced, stored in a retrieval system, or transmitted in any form or by any means – electronic, mechanical, photocopy, recording, or any other – except for brief quotations in printed reviews, without the prior permission of the publisher.

*Priority*ONE Publications
P. O. Box 34722 / Detroit, MI 48234
E-mail: info@priorityonebooks.com
URL: http://www.priorityonebooks.com
1 (313) 312-5318

ISBN 13: 978-1-933972-32-9
ISBN 10:   1-933972-32-7

Edited by Patricia A. Hicks
Cover and interior design by PriorityONE Publications

Printed in the United States of America

TABLE OF CONTENTS

ACKNOWLEDGEMENTS 5

PREFACE 6

ABSTRACT 7

LIST OF TABLES 8

Chapter

    I.   Introduction 9
             Purpose, Framework, Scope and Literature Review

    II.   Related Literature Review and Study Dimensions of the Study 26

    III.   Methodology 42
             Study Design and Study Population

    IV.   Field Study Results and Analysis 69

    V.   Conclusions and Implications 72

    VI.   Appendices 73

    VII.   References 84

    VIII.   About the Author 89

A Descriptive Examination of the Effects of Spiritual Freedom of Persons Serving Life Sentences on Their Communication Climates

Brenda Simuel Jackson

Dissertation

Submitted to the Office of the Academic Dean of

Jacksonville Theological Seminary,

Jacksonville, Florida

In partial fulfillment of the requirements for a degree of

Doctor of Philosophy in Divinity

2013

Major: Prison Ministry

Approved by Academic Dean, Dr. Harold Vick, II

Acknowledgements

Without the support and spiritual assistance of the following persons, completion of this study would not have been possible: Chaplain John Dorris and Sterling Overton, a past Director of Michigan Department of Corrections, who made it possible for me to have access to the study population; Elder Arnoldine Lancaster, Brenda M. Rudolph and the prayer conference team of BSJ Christian Seminars, Inc., who kept me lifted in prayer, my facilitator, Dr. Queen Kyles, who always had words of encouragement and facilitated the removal of obstacles. I must acknowledge the most important person, My Lord, who made all this possible.

Preface

Free in a Cage

© 2012 Brenda Simuel Jackson

Locked in a cage, but I'm free as I can be through the Holy Spirit Who lives in me.

Having the mind of Christ helps me stay focused on the positive aspects of my life.

Although the C/O tells me when I can get up in the morning, the Holy Spirit gives me peace enabling me to see each day dawning.

During the shake down, my small space was no longer my own, but the kindness through the Holy Spirit allowed humility to remind me, the space was only on loan.

I had signed up for the seminar, but my name was not on the call-out list. The self-control in me produced a calmness and not a fist.

I can interact freely with inmates, the Chaplain, and COs because my faith directs my tone and communication as I go.

My body is locked in a cage, but the Spirit in me controls my mind, emotions, and actions giving me freedom in every aspect of the way.

I learned that how I wait is a choice given to me, and when I don't quench the Spirit's power, my choices set me free.

Locked in a cage? I am free through the love of the One who gave His life for me, giving me a freedom that comes from above and is in eternity.

Abstract

      The purpose of this descriptive analysis is to analyze the relationship between a positive communication climate and one's spiritual freedom. The target environment is prison, and the target population is inmates serving life sentences or a period of time covering a major portion of their lives such as twenty years. Inmates assessed their spirituality and spiritual freedom through a questionnaire which was analyzed using principles of a descriptive and content analyses. The questionnaire was based on Galatians 5:22-26, "Fruit of the Spirit," and 6:16, used as evidence of being spirit-controlled, and Romans 8:1-4 indicating that believers in Christ are controlled by the Holy Spirit. Interviews were conducted with 32% of the participants in the survey. The interviews were used to provide a reliability measure to descriptions of spirituality and spiritual freedoms indicated via surveys. Professional Counselors, experienced in working with inmates and/or ex-offenders were interviewed to provide assessment behaviors observed relative to spirituality and positive communication interactions. The analysis results confirmed a positive communication climate and the exercise of spiritual freedoms describe the relationships and the communication environment of Lifers who deemed themselves to be Spiritually controlled.

List of Charts and Tables

Table 1	Spiritual Fruit	13
Table 2	Power of Words	33
Table 3	Respondents in the Study	43
Table 4	Self Described Spirituality	44
Table 5	Themes for Spiritual Friends	45
Table 6	Spiritual Designations/Themes of Friends	45
Table 7	Behavior Designating Spiritual Friends	47
Table 8	A Trusting Climate	48
Table 9	Disclosure	54
Table 10	Verbal Conflict	57

INTRODUCTION

Purpose, Framework, Scope and Literature Review:

Romans 8:2 states:

"because through Christ Jesus the law of the Spirit of life set me free from the law of sin and death." (NIV)

Galatians 5:1a and 5:16 say:

"It is for freedom that Christ has set us free…. So I say, live by the Spirit, and you will not gratify the desires of the sinful nature." (NIV)

There are several forms of freedom: freedom from persecution, freedom from stress, freedom from emotional distress, freedom from physical illness, and freedom to make choices. These freedoms fit into two basic types: physical and spiritual (Youngblood, Bruce, & Harrison, 1995). Physical freedom provides the liberty to go where one wishes to go, do what one wishes to do, and say what one wishes to say. Liberty implies power over one's surroundings and environment. The sanctions in our criminal justice system for criminal offenders is often incarceration, the taking away or restriction of one's physical freedoms, negating the exercise of liberties associated with physical freedom. Incarceration limits the establishment of relations, often causing breaks in existing relationships.

According to Richards (1991), freedom as a concept in the New Testament is spiritual and relational (p. 294). Spiritual freedom is therefore based on a relationship.

Characteristics of freedom of a Christian include abilities such as:

- Acting in love
- Sharing of joy
- Promoting peace (Richards, 1987, p. 910)

Exhibiting these characteristics is relational behavior. Paul describes the affirmation of freedom as a response to God's call to follow the goodness of Christ (Galatians 5:13-6:18, NIV). Paul further says:

"Now the Lord is the Spirit, and where the Spirit of the Lord is, there is freedom." (2 Corinthians 3:17, NIV).

It is the relationship with Jesus that initiates freedom. Spiritual freedom is based on knowing truth, and Jesus is truth. Jesus sets people free (John 8:32). Spiritual freedom breaks the bondage of "sin"; it is choosing to serve God. Choice is spiritual freedom regardless of the physical surroundings. The nature of this freedom is found in Galatians 5:1-13. A person is freed from choices that produce hatred, jealousy, and fits of rage which are all characteristics that break relationships.

Spiritual freedom is enabled by the Holy Spirit. The Holy Spirit will enable us to act in ways contrary to our natural inclinations, but we must select this direction.

Galatians 5:16 teaches that if we surrender ourselves to the Spirit, to let Him guide or control us, then the Spirit will see to it that we do not gratify our sinful desires. Spiritual freedom results in being in harmony and unity with God's commands (Galatians 5:16, 17, 22, 25).

Kelleman (2004) indicates that "persons who exhibit spiritual freedom have spiritual friendships that start with people" (p.105). These spiritual friendships are based on understanding those who are having problems, their use of biblical approaches to diagnose the problem to develop solutions to the problem and to use methods of intervention in to the situation (p. 105).

Clinton and Staub (2010) expand this concept by indicating that spiritual freedoms require community.

Hurting people who experience God's love, are empowered by God's Spirit, and what is shared by God's people causes their hearts to be full to overflowing (p. 193). Spiritual freedom requires developing a spiritual life. A spiritual life has spiritual habits (p. 172). Such habits include:

- Bible Study
- Prayer
- Silence
- Solitude

- Service

Spiritual freedom demonstrates freedom from anxiety; one can respond thoughtfully to difficulties (p. 186). Clinton and Staub (2010) indicate that:

> Coming to see others as capable of loving us, yet not feeling worthy of love, can lead us to seek relationships rather than material possessions to calm our anxiousness (p. 187).

Prison and freedom appear to be contradictory concepts when viewed from the perspectives of choice, relationships, and not being bound. A quote from Casarjean (1996) provides logic that breaks the fallacy of arguing from a perceived false premise, that persons who are incarcerated are free (p. 228).

> Although prison may look like a spiritual wasteland, no outer gate, wall, or fence can ever keep you from a connection with the spiritual.

Aday (2003), reporting on the study of Koenig, summarized the results by indicating:

> Religious background, belief activities, experience and intrinsic religiosity are important to the adjustment and behavior of prisoners (p. 132).

Religiosity is viewed as those involved in prayer, scripture reading, and involvement in religious activities. The study which involved 96 male inmates in a Federal institution, ages 50 and over, concluded that religious motivation served as an important factor in reducing emotional duress (p.132).

Cases which demonstrate spiritual freedom during incarceration include inmate Charles Watson. Watson has been incarcerated over 35 years, and has spent most of that time sharing his faith with other prisoners. His spiritual freedom involves freely sharing his faith. Mr. Watson has no possibility of parole; therefore, there is no particular personal gain such as physical freedom for dedicating his life to prison ministry (Johnson, 2011).

A chaplain, ministering on death row in a Florida State prison in Starke, reported that persons on death row, who had given their lives to God, were at peace and ready to die (p. 162). Chaplain Khoo reports how he walked inmates to the gallows. In Singapore hanging was the method of carrying out the death penalty. Khoo said he could see the difference in inmates who were Christian; they had peace and calmness in comparison to others who were bitter and angry (p. 163). This researcher ministered in the Kabwe Prison, in Lusaka Zambia, 2011-2012, to inmates on death row. They freely participated in worship services. The Spirit was of praise and rejoicing. Several had been on death row for over 20 years.

An article by Daniel Rebant (2012) defines spiritual freedom as the soul-deep liberation of those who live by the Spirit, not by human ego or worldly values.

Purpose:

The study question for this investigation involves what are the effects of Spiritual Freedom on the environment of the incarcerated. For purposes of this study, Spiritual Freedom means being controlled by the Holy Spirit which is evidenced by exhibiting in one's daily life the Fruit of the Spirit; love, joy, peace, patience, kindness, goodness, faithfulness, gentleness, and self-control (Galatians 5:22-26). Spiritual fruit is evidence of a transformed character; it is evidence of a character united with the Lord; it is divine power from within. It is being controlled by the Spirit (Romans 7:4-5).

Fruitfulness is rooted in an interpersonal relationship with Jesus where one's behavior exhibits living by His Word (Richards, p. 299; Ephesians 4:1-4).

Framework and Scope:

What is the Fruit of the Spirit?

Out of the overflow of the heart, the mouth speaks (Luke 6:45). Spiritual fruit is identified by how and what a person speaks. A person's character is betrayed by their words. It is known from a Biblical perspective that every word out of one's mouth is serious for God

(Matthew 12:36). Our words acquit us and our words can condemn us (Matthew 12:37). Our words are an aspect of our spiritual fruit. June Hart (2004) stresses that being filled by the Spirit is being controlled by the Spirit (p. 7). "Being indwelled is simply the Holy Spirit taking residence in us, becoming alive in us; indwelled is a once occurrence, but being filled is on-going, repeated occurrences" (Ryrie, 1972, p. 83). Being Spirit-controlled according to Ryrie results in four basic characteristics:

1. Christlikeness, for the fruit of the Spirit is Christlikeness,
2. Worship and praise, for one has a heart that sings and is thankful,
3. Submissiveness, as one has relationships that promote harmony, and
4. Service to God. (p. 84-85)

The following Tables provide a Biblical survey of the Fruit of Spirit.

Table 1 – Spiritual Fruit (Galatians 5:22-23)

Fruit	Scriptures	Descriptions	Applications
Love (αγαπε)	Galatians 5:22	Produced by the Holy Spirit	Living Christlike; love is the foundation of grace.
	1 John 4:7-8, & 12	God is Love	Whoever loves has been born of God; whoever does not love, does not know God
	Romans 5:5; 12:9-10	God's love ministered to the believer by the Holy Spirit; there is sincerity, humility, commitment	Be fervent in service for the Lord; show social concern for one another; have no hypocrisy.

Table 1 – Spiritual Fruit continued

Fruit	Scriptures	Descriptions	Applications
Love (αγαπε) continued	1 Corinthians 13:4-7	Equals patience, kindness; does not envy, does not boast, is not proud, is not rude, is not self-seeking; is not easily angered;	
	1 Corinthians 13:5-7	Keeps no record of wrongs, does not like evil, has joy with truth; protects, trusts, is hopeful, has perseverance.	When wronged does not retaliate, does not seek self-satisfaction, does not rush to litigation, watches how communication occurs in service, remains steadfast even in unpleasant situations, demonstrates God's love, and does not seek to do harm.
	2 Corinthians 8:24	Love has action.	Giving to those in need.
	Galatians 5:13-14	Serving others not self.	Guard against self-righteousness.
	1 Peter 4:8	Love strenuously, sacrificing for others, and accepting their faults	Sacrifice for others regardless of their faults.

Table 1a – Fruit of the Spirit

Fruit	Scriptures	Description	Application
Joy (χαρα)	Galatians 5:22	Inner rejoicing because of a relationship with Christ.	The joy of Christ is shown through obedience.
	John 15:9-11	See Galatians 5:22	See Galatians 5:22
	Luke 10:21	Jesus brings joy through the Holy Spirit	Joy is produced from within and is not the external signs we see of laughter.
	Psalm 16:11	Joy is in the presence of God.	Live a life that leads to God's eternal Presence.
	Deuteronomy 16:15	Joy is a relationship with God.	
	1 Chronicles 16:1-36	Joy in God's provisions; joy in God's deliverance. David rejoices by thanking God through burnt offerings and fellowship offerings.	Celebration of our salvation, and of God's blessings.
	Psalm 19:8a	Joy is God's Word.	Righteousness brings inner joy which we receive from the Word of God.
	Psalm 119:14	Obedience to God's Word brings joy.	Our richness is in God's Word.
	Romans 14:16-17	The Kingdom of God includes joy in the Holy Spirit and does not allow our good to be spoken about as evil.	Joy is salvation.

Table 1a - Fruit of the Spirit continued

Fruit	Scriptures	Description	Application
Joy (χαρα) continued	Acts 16:34	The jailer was filled with joy because he and his family believed.	The time of testing our faith is to build perseverance and brings joy.
	2 Corinthians 7:2-4	In times of trouble, Paul continues to have joy.	
	Philippians 1:25, 26; 2:1-2	Faith brings joy; being united with Christ brings joy.	Encouragement because of one's relationship with Christ.

Table 1b - Fruit of the Spirit

Fruit	Scriptures	Description	Application
Peace (ειπηνη)	Galatians 5:22	A gift of Christ.	Inner repose even in adverse circumstances.
	Romans 1:7	See Galatians 5:22	See Galatians 5:22
	1 Corinthians 1:3	See Galatians 5:22	See Galatians 5:22
	Ephesians 2:14-18	Peace is unity.	In Christ, there is no division; all believers have been reconciled back to God; there is one Spirit.
	1 Corinthians 4:33	God is not a God of disorder but of peace.	Through Christ there is order and harmony.
	Mark 5:34	Being healed is receiving peace.	Enjoy being content and rest in God's healing.

Table 1b - Fruit of the Spirit continued

Fruit	Scriptures	Description	Application
Peace (ειπηνη) continued	2 Timothy 2:22	Pursue righteousness, faith, love, and peace, then call on the Lord from a pure heart.	Peace is a commitment to harmony.
	Colossians 3:12-15	The peace of Christ rules our character.	The attitude of peace is compassion, kindness, humility, gentleness, and patience which are the results of the Holy Spirit and causes us to forgive as Christ forgave us.
	Matthew 10:34	Peace with Christ causes conflict with others.	Christ ia first in our lives, peace with Christ is conflict with those against Christ.
	John 14:27	Peace of Christ brings inner peace that lets the believer face danger and suffering without fear.	In unity with Christ, there is no fear of the future; His peace is in us.
	John 16:33	The believer has inner peace in spite of the trouble in the world; he has victory in Christ.	We can face the troubles of this world knowing our future is secure.

Table 1c - Fruit of The Spirit

Fruit	Scriptures	Description	Application
Longsuffering (μακροθυμια)	Galatians 5:22	One forebears when provoked.	One does not retaliate when wronged.
	Romans 2:4	This provides the opportunity for repentance.	Longsuffering provides time for change from wrong actions to God's way.

Table 1d - Fruit of The Spirit

Fruit	Scriptures	Description	Application
Kindness (χρηστοησ)	Galatians 5:22	Opposite of judgment.	Acceptance of the benevolence of God, His salvation.
	Ephesians 2:7	God's Grace.	We walk in God's grace daily.
	Titus 3:4	God saved us because of His mercy. He saved us through the washing of, rebirth of, and renewal by the Holy Spirit Whom He poured out on us through Jesus Christ.	God's moral goodness in us enables us to be kind to others.
	Luke 6:35	Loving and being kind tour enemies; lending with no expectation of a return.	We follow Jesus Who is kind to the ungrateful and the wicked.
	Ephesians 4:32	Forgiving.	Through forgiving each other we are kind to one another.

Table 1e - Fruit of the Spirit

Fruit	Scriptures	Descriptions	Applications
Goodness (Αγαθωσυνη)	Galatians 5:22	Morally honorable and reaching out to others.	Doing good to others even when not deserved.
	Luke 8:8	Being good soil.	Having a character with beneficial effects.

Table 1f - Fruit of The Spirit

Fruit	Scriptures	Description	Application
Faith (Πιστιο)	Galatians 5:22	Justification through Christ.	A quality of trustworthiness.
	Romans 325; 2 Corinthians 1:24	Firm persuasion or conviction on hearing the Gospel.	Faith in One Who is reliable, causes us to be faithful servants.
	John 1:12; 2 Corinthians 5:7	Surrender to Christ and gain a relationship with God.	Our conduct exhibits our surrender.
	Matthew 24:45; 25:21-23	Servanthood.	Good stewardship.
	1 Corinthians 4:2	Be faithful to the trust given to us.	Be committed servants.

Table 1g - Fruit of the Spirit

Fruit	Scriptures	Descriptions	Applications
Meekness (Πραστησ)	Galatians 5:22; James 1:21	Humbly accept the Word planted in us.	Submissiveness to God's Word.
	Matthew 5:5	The humble are already blessed.	Recognize our relation to God, our lowly estate when we are compared to God. We must know our position.
	1 Peter 3:4	Inner beauty of a quiet spirit.	Submissiveness.
	James 3:13	Learned humility.	Use wisdom and understanding in acting humbly.
	1 Peter 3:15	Speaking in gentleness.	Show respect when defending reasons for your hope.

Table 1h - Fruit of The Spirit

Fruit	Scriptures	Descriptions	Applications
Self-Control (Εγκρατεια)	Galatians 5:23	Self-mastery.	Curbing desires of the flesh.
	Titus 1:8	Disciplined.	Inner strength to control desires.

The summary descriptions and applications of Table 1, a-h, are based on definitions in Richards (2004) and Vine, Unger, & White (1985), and Bauer, Arndt, Gingrich & Danker (1958).

The impact of exercising spiritual freedom (fruit of the Spirit), is the development of a climate conducive to building positive interpersonal relations with others in an environment where interpersonal relations are restricted. A positive communication which flows from the power of spiritual fruit has the following characteristics:

1. Trust
2. Disclosure
3. Absence of conflict
4. Brotherly love (philios)

What is a Communication Climate?

The communication climate is the emotional attitude within an intrapersonal (inner self), and in an interpersonal relationship (self and another). It is responsiveness to situations. Floyd (2011) reports that researchers define communication climate as the emotional tone of a relationship (p. 338). Wood (2002) defines the climate for interpersonal communication as an overall feeling or emotional mood between people (p. 264). A positive communication has beneficial results for various settings: family, friendships, workplaces, and educational settings (Floyd, p. 338). This investigation adds to this paradigm the prison as a setting for interpersonal relationships. Positive communication exhibits behaviors that indicate how much another person is valued (p 338). Relations are strengthened within a positive communication situation. A positive communication climate is non-judgmental and non-evaluative (p. 342). Seay (2002) provides an example of the impact of peace (intrapersonal condition) and interpersonal relations.

> Bobby, age 62, began serving his time at the age of 12. He learned of Christ from the Chaplain, and a difference was produced in his life producing real freedom and inner peace. This peace brought about a calm in his relations with his loved ones (p.80).

In the context of spirituality, Floyd defines communication as a method of expressing and sharing spiritual ideas (p.8). Spirituality requires a communication outlet.

Descriptions of prison settings do not depict a positive communication environment. Santos (2006) describes the prison setting for those with a minimum sentence of twenty-six (26) years as survival of the fittest (p.28). Prisoners develop a survival strategy which includes building alliances with other prisoners. This alliance is based on providing skills to those who need skills possessed by each other. In this concept, communication among prisoners which is non-threatening is because it leads to goal achievement. The effects of life in prison have negative impact on communication and on the environment of communication. According to Pierce (2006, p.65), the effects of life imprisonment include:

- Loneliness,
- Degradation,
- Boredom,
- Less Caring Attitude,
- Loss of control,
- Loss of individuality, and
- Loss of self esteem

These characteristics are opposites of the Fruit of the Spirit. Those doing hard time in a maximum security facility behave in one of the following ways:

- They live in a fantasy world, or
- They engage in a meaningful, time-consuming activity (p.71)

    The physical surroundings may create a negative communication climate. A view of Leavenworth gives a vivid picture. Some cells, according to Williams (2000), are 4' by 8', made of steel and concrete. There are several levels of cells and those housed on the upper levels are caught in a heat trap. The sinks are made so water trickles down the side of the bowl with no way to capture the water. At night in Kansas, the air is stifling. Men scream all kinds of obscenities all night long (p. 134-6). The outside of the facility is likened to a castle. The walls consist of huge stones stacked upon one another. Guard towers are spaced evenly around the castle. There are eight wings with the control area in the center (p. 134).

In areas of "supermaximum" security, the design is to restrict communication through isolation and to restrict inmate interaction. Inmates in such security (ADX) pass at least twenty-three (23) hours of every day in isolation on a concrete bunk or other similar articles (Santos, p. 47-48). Violence, according to Santos, is part of high security facilities (p. 50-52). In a Federal penitentiary, stabbings are the norm, and the manufacturing of weapons is to be expected. There is a class structure of manipulators, and manipulated; the dominators and the dominated; as well as the exploiters and the exploited (p. 29). Vengeance killings were described as a norm, including the killing of guards (p. 37).

Research Questions:

The research questions are:

A. What is the impact of spiritual freedom on persons incarcerated for life or a significant portion, i.e. 20 years, of their life?

B. Is there a relationship between spiritual freedom and a positive communication environment of inmates, where communication is usually guarded due to environmental pressures of the incarceration?

Primary Hypothesis:

It is hypothesized that the impact of exercising spiritual freedom is the development of a climate conducive to building positive interpersonal relations within an environment which restricts interpersonal relationships.

The Role of Trust within the Communication Climate:

Level of trust is an organizational attitude and an important variable within the communication climate. Sanford's study (1972) demonstrated that a trusting climate has openness and honesty (p.23). A trusting climate relies on the communicative behavior of another person to achieve a desired objective in a risky situation (Sanford, Hunt, and Bracey, 1976, p. 228). Distrust has a negative impact leading to communication failures (Likert, 1967, p. 45-46). Trust is defined as having the following aspects:

1. **Credibility of the communicator:** Credibility is defined as expertness where the communicator is perceived to be a source

of valid information and trustworthiness where there is confidence in the communicator's intent (Hovland, Irving, Kelly, 1965, p.29).

2. **Lack of suspicion:** The communicator is perceived as having no ulterior or hidden motives within the communication process. The study by Hovland-Mandell indicated that where the communicator was perceived as having something to gain, trustworthiness was perceived differently than in situations where such motives were non-existent (p. 29).

3. **Freedom from fear to discuss:** With authority, the problems and difficulties one has are discussed without having it held against one (Hovland, et al. p.29).

4. **Disclosure of Information:** Disclosure is characterized by feelings of low risk, as defined by Fritz Steel (Wheeless, 1978, p. 143).

According to Lawrence Wheeless, risky behavior is dependent behavior and such behavior is based on favorable perceptions of others in terms of trustworthiness and character. This concept is supported by Bridges (1970), Pearce (1974), Hovland and Mandell (1952), Hovland, Janis, and Kelly (1953), and Wheeless and Gratz (1975-1977), (Wheeless, 143).

Related Literature and Further Dimensions of the Study

Fruit of The Spirit and One's Character:

> And if the Spirit of Him who raised Jesus from the dead is living in you, He who raised Christ from the dead will also give life to your mortal bodies through His spirit, who lives in you (Romans 8:11, NIV).

> For you did not receive a spirit that makes you a slave again to fear, but you received the spirit of sonship… (8:15a NIV).

The fruit is God's expectation for the believer's character. This is how Billy Graham (1978), described the Fruit of the Spirit (p. 182). Halloman (1994) stresses the vital relationship between God's Spirit and His Word in the believer's life. It is this relationship that gives the believer freedom from guilt and freedom to serve God.

Ephesians 6:6 (NIV) clearly indicates that doing the Will of God is from the heart, therefore, by the Spirit (Bruce, 1977, p. 199). Halloman's reliance on Romans 8:9 indicate an agreement that having the Fruit of the Spirit is an indication of being Spirit-controlled. Graham goes further by indicating man cannot achieve godliness, spiritual fruit without the Spirit. It is the Fruit of the Spirit that gets one through difficulties and hardships (Graham, 181; Romans 8:29). Graham uses the extended analogy I Psalm 1 to explain the results of having spiritual fruit, as well as its relationship to and application of God's Word. Graham divides the Fruit of the Spirit into three clusters:

- **Love, joy, and peace** are described as our relationship with God (p. 187). Our prayers, praying in the Spirit, and praying God's Words and Will are indicators of this cluster of fruit.
- **Patience, kindness, and goodness** are our relationship with others. Being quick to anger, and being rude are indications that this aspect of the fruit is still maturing and may need

pruning. When the Spirit controls a person, the results are patience, kindness, and goodness (p. 195).

- **Faithfulness, gentleness, and self-control** are an inward relationship. These are indicators of the inner self, our attitudes (p. 187). Spiritual maturity is seen in this third cluster in the following ways: responsibility is accepted and commitment to worship is maintained (p. 203). It is this cluster that produces meekness, which is quiet strength in a hostile environment (p. 206).

Examples of the third cluster as mature are:

a. Does not get defensive when feelings are hurt (Matthew 26:51, 52).
b. Does not crave preeminence (3 John 9), and
c. Does not seek recognition (2 Timothy 3:8) (p. 207).

One can control his/her thoughts and actions. Spiritual freedom is gained through applying God's truth to our lives.

Guerero describes how the Fruit of the Spirit communicates comfort and support in non-verbal methods such as: hugs, pats, eye control, facial expressions, and permitting close distance in one's space (p. 283). This sets a tone for a positive communication climate.

Spirituality:

A person's view of spirituality is probably related to one's personal belief system. For this researcher, spirituality is rooted in faith in the Savior, Jesus Christ and His Gospel, with the authority of God's Word, the Bible. One's spirituality determines one's life style states Dr. Gary Collins (2001).

> "True spirituality requires guidance by the Holy Spirit of God and the Truth of the Word of God" (p. 234).

Spirituality may be synonymous with holiness. Our spirituality causes us to be relational in the community of faith first, and then with those in the world. The fruit of the Spirit is not for intrapersonal relationship but for interpersonal relationship. Spirituality is interpersonal.

The Medical Center of the University of Maryland, in an article on Spirituality (2011), defined spirituality from a different perspective.

> A belief in a power operating in the universe that is greater than oneself; a sense of interconnectedness with all living creatures, and an awareness of the purpose and meaning of life and the development of personal, absolute values. It's the way you find meaning, hope, comfort, and inner peace (p. 2).

The writer of Hebrews 12:14-15 says that believers are to make every effort to live in peace with all men and to be holy, without holiness no one will see the Lord. See to it that no one misses the grace of God and that no bitter root grows up to cause trouble and defile man. Bitter fruit is what causes strife among men. We are reminded by Dr. Collins that:

> … the Holy Spirit, the developer of fruit in our lives, changes us to live in accordance with God's Word (p. 118). We are further reminded that Jesus sent His disciples into the world. He did not take them out of the world (John 17:14-15, NIV)

Casarjean (1996, p. 224) states "that it is the spirituality of the inmate that changes the inmate in a positive way while living in a culture which may deny the spiritual. It is through the Spirit that an inmate becomes more insightful, forgiving, yet confident in being able to overcome challenges." Spirituality therefore can increase true self-awareness of who one is, and of one's true existence.

"Interaction guided by spirituality provides security based on trust, and truth is then spoken with love" (Clinton & Staub, p. 189). According to Casarjean, spirituality brings about meaningful experiences that achieve understanding (p. 229). Floyd indicates spirituality is an aspect of one's existence (p. 7), and therefore, is a major factor in determining one's values and moral concepts. As spirituality is a part of our identity, our attitudes, our values, it is expressed through our communication. Our communication includes attitudes of optimism and hope (Maryland University, p. 1). Our interpersonal relationships move us to wholeness. "There is a need to share one's space with someone who will give a definitive perspective in times of confusion, and who will laugh with us as well as cry with us" (Clinton & Staub, p. 169).

The self-insights of spirituality result in spiritual truths about the self (Casarjean, p. 237-8). These truths include:

- You are loved.
- You are worthy of respect and acceptance.
- Your true nature is fundamentally good and beautiful.
- You *are* needed in helping to heal the world.

Spirituality is hope. It changes denial of circumstances of grief from the loss of freedom through incarceration to hope engendered by the fruit of the Spirit, and that provides strength to accept, 'I am incarcerated.' Spirituality is faith that has produced a spiritual change in one's life. Spirituality builds a Christlike character according to Billy Graham (p. 181).

A Spiritual Lifestyle:

Spirituality is not jailhouse religion which Johnson (2011), defines as "the sudden desperate piety of an inmate who's up against it and hopes that God will somehow bail him out" (p. 154). Spirituality provides a life in accordance with Romans 8:29,

> *"For those God foreknew He also predestined to be conformed to the likeness of His Son, that He might be the firstborn among many brothers."*

Siang states, He wants us to walk in the Spirit, day by day, year after year, for a lifetime to be built up until we all reach unity in faith and knowledge of the Son of God, until we become mature. The spiritual environment includes contentment (Siang-Yang, p. 179), health derived from applying God's wisdom (Proverbs 3:6-8), and giving spiritual items priority with sincerity (Lieth, 2011).

Paul writes in 1 Corinthians 2:4,

> My message and my preaching were not with wise and persuasive words, but with a demonstration of the Spirit's power....

2 Corinthians 3:17, 18:

> Now the Lord is the Spirit, and where the Spirit of the Lord is, there is freedom. And we, who with unveiled faces all reflect the Lord's glory, are being transformed into His likeness with ever-increasing glory, which comes from the Lord, who is the Spirit. (NIV).

Based on Paul's writings, Dr. Collins says transformation through the indwelling Holy Spirit gives freedom and spiritual power (p. 158).

In a study of the Inner Change Freedom Initiative Program (a prison rehabilitation process), Johnson reports (p.153) how the faith based environments, programs with spiritual transformation, have a positive impact on offender rehabilitation. Spirituality transforms relationships, in a positive direction, giving freedom and power to influence the environment in which one lives (Collins, p. 158).

The inmate's spiritual lifestyle shows an increase in the participation of religious programs and services. Casarjean reports "increased meditation, prayer, reflecting on religious experiences, spiritual and inspirational writings" (p. 228). Aday reports such religious activities help older inmates adjust to the prison culture (p. 133). Spiritual practices tend to improve coping skills and social support (University of Maryland, p. 1). Coping techniques of the spiritual include Bible study and worship.

Lifestyle qualities which impact the communication climate, as previously defined, are spiritual in nature. These qualities include:

- Honesty
- Truth and Faith
- Tolerance
- Gentleness/Kindness

- Generosity
- Patience
- Forgiveness
- Justice
- Love (Casarjean, p. 239-242)

Programs such as the Inner Change Freedom Initiative based on Christian principles, are providing an environment and curriculum that are Biblically based, and transforms the communication climate (Johnson, p. 153).

Overcoming Prisonization:

The effects of spirituality are not key areas of investigation for the Criminal Justice Department; however, projections are made regarding the probable impact imprisonment will have on the characters of the inmates. The hypothesis of some researchers, regarding character change of lifers as stated by Sapsford (1983), is that the behavior of the inmate will deteriorate because of confinement and the loss of freedom of actions (p.24). The researchers projected that behavior will change from active or aggressive to passive; the person will become withdrawn and indifferent (p. 25). The hypothesis is based on the concept of the effects of deprivation, and a change from independent behavior where one's behavior was based on personal motives to an environment of dependency on circumstances of which one has no control. The study, Life I project, involved 60 inmates convicted of homicide and serving life imprisonment. The variables examined for deterioration included:

a. Depression
b. Hopelessness
c. Anxiety
d. Introversion
e. Emotionality
f. Apathy
g. Dependence on staff

h. Motivation to succeed

i. Interest in outside contacts

j. Orientation to time

k. General psychiatric state (p. 45).

Of the above stated variables, seven are viewed as variables with a direct impact on the direction of the tone in the communication climate:

a. Depression

b. Hopelessness

c. Anxiety

d. Introversion

e. Apathy

f. Motivation to succeed

g. Interests in outside contacts.

The main outcome of the longitudinal analysis is that prisoners did not deteriorate, because they found ways of coming to terms with the prison environment and using it for their own purposes (p. 63). Man defines himself in relation to the world by a set of expectations as to what he can or cannot do and what he/she is free to do; from these a hierarchical model is developed about what one is able to do. Anxiety is generated when the behavior doesn't fit the model (p. 38). The results of the second phase of the project found that lifers adapt. The adaptation tools are coping and choice of meekness and in how to cope (p. 63).

Another aspect of prisonization, according to Pierce (p. 82-83), is victimization resulting from isolation panic. To overcome isolation, inmates seek social contact and pursue constructive activities such as pastoral counseling and visitation (p. 82-83). Spiritual communication is a coping mechanism. Sachs (2012) says that enemies are turned into friends through spiritual communication (p. 500). Such communication sees all parties to the process as being in the image of God (p. 510). Spiritual communication is defined as a type of prayer and can only be engaged when the individual is in a true relationship with God. One's conversation becomes the compelling element. The speech is viewed as having more power than physical power. The power is described in Proverbs 18:21, "The tongue has the power of life and death, and those who live it will eat its fruit" (NIV). The following Table provides an overview of Proverbial wisdom regarding the power of conversation through words.

Table 2 - The Power of Words

Scriptures in Proverbs	Words of Live	Scriptures in Proverbs	Words of Death
4:20	Listen closely	3:30	False accusations
8:6	Things of worth; what is right	4:24	Perverseness; corrupt talk
8:7	What is true	6:16-19	Lying tongues, false witness
8:8	What is just	10:11	Violent speech
8:9	Gentle answers	10:18	Slander
12:6	Integrity/ rescues	12:6	Killing words / draws blood
12:18	Wise words heal	12:18	Reckless words pierce life
16:24	Pleasant words heal	16:28	Gossip separates friends
22:11	Gracious speech promotes friends	20:19	Gossip destroys confidence
25:11	A word properly spoken is like a jewel (precious)	25:23	Sly tongue brings anger

Communication Climate and a Trusting Attitude:

It has been demonstrated that trust is an important variable in the communication climate. The construct of trust as an attitude within the communication environment consists of the following factors:

- Credibility of the communicator

- Lack of suspicion of the communicator
- Freedom from fear to discuss with the communicator
- Disclosure of information to the communicator.

This construct was greatly influenced by a theory and studies of interpersonal trust of Kim Griffin (1967), as well as theories and studies of disclosure, primarily from Lawrence R. Wheeless, provider of a large part of the following information. Giffin describes the behavior of a trusting person as:

- A person who is relying upon something.
- This something relied upon may be an object, an event, or a person.
- Something is risked by the trusting person.
- The desired goal is not perceived as certain.
- The trusting person has some degree of confidence in the object of his/her trust.

Based on these features, Giffin defines trust as:

> …reliance upon the characteristics of an object or the occurrence of an event, or the behavior of a person in order to achieve a desired but uncertain objective in a risky situation (p. 104).

Based on the concept of T.M. Newcomb's, *An Approach to the Study of Communication Acts* (1953), Giffin conceptualizes the relationship between a trusting person and the object of trust as an orientation, and thus as an attitude in the broad meaning of the term.

Newcomb defined orientation as equivalent to attitude in *Psychological Review*, 149-150.

Aspects of interpersonal trust are constructs to the concepts of trust used by this researcher:

- Source credibility defined as Ethos by Aristotle.

- Psychological safety and acceptance as prescribed by Carl Rogers (1961), and
- A perceived supporting climate as explored by J.R. Gibb (1961 & 1964).

The idea of psychological safety is closely related to this researcher's use of the second and the third elements of the definition of trust as an attitude, lack of suspicion, and freedom from fear to discuss. Carl Rogers (1961) indicates that the only way in which a relationship can have reality is by being genuine, which involves the willingness to express in words and behavior the feelings and attitudes which exist.

Such a reality can exist when there is acceptance of the person. Acceptance is defined as:

> ...a warm regard for him or her as a person of unconditional self-worth, of value, no matter what his or her condition, his or her behavior, or his or her feelings. It means a respect and liking for him or her as a separate person... (p. 33-34).

Within a group situation, Tannenbaum found an increase in flexibility, openness, and willingness to listen; people were open to new ideas and tried to understand and accept such ideas (Rogers, p. 299 -230). Such climate of safety is defined by Gibb as supportive (p. 107).

Specific data relative to the impact of fear within the communication relationship (as related to persuasion) is discussed by Hovland, Janis, and Kelly, (p. 56-91), and is based on their findings that fear within the environment may cause a rejection of the communicator, a rejection of his/her ideas, a perception of being manipulated, and an arousal of aggressiveness. Wheeless' discussion further states:

> The depth of the disclosure would be a function of the self-perceived intimacy of the information, topic revealed, the honesty of those revelations, the accuracy with which the individual perceives himself and is subsequently capable of verbalizing those perceptions, and the conscious intent

(willingness) of the individual to make self-revealing disclosures (p. 338).

The depth of disclosure ties in with factors of freedom from fear to discuss and lack of suspicion. True fellowship is the result of freedom to be oneself, freedom to remove masks, and freedom to be honest with one another (Siang Tan, 1997). This requires a trusting environment. True fellowship, continues Dr. Siang-Tan, is the willingness to be open with others about personal problems, needs, and to risk rejection. Floyd says self-disclosure is a gradual process (p.97).

All communication is not self-disclosure. Floyd says there are two conditions which must be present to qualify as a disclosure:

- There must be a deliberate action/intention to share information about self.
- There is the belief that the information is true (p. 95).

In conclusion, self-disclosure is intentional and truthful. Self-disclosure is usually reciprocal; shared information is an expectation. Wood (2002) describes the communication climate as allowing greater knowledge about the persons involved (p. 289). The situation produces increased trust.

There are risks to self-disclosure:

- Rejection
- Chance of obligating others
- Hurt to others
- Violation of other's privacy (Floyd, p 101).

There are two types of climates as outlined by Woods (p. 286). There is a defensive climate and a supportive climate. Supportive climates contribute to positive interaction. The benefits of self-disclosure in a positive climate are:

- Enhancement of relationships and trust
- Reciprocity
- Emotional release

- Assistance of others (Floyd p. 99-100).

In measuring self-disclosure, Wheeless and Gratz used thirty-two Likert type statements to measure self-reported self-disclosure on dimensions of frequency, duration, intimacy, honesty, accuracy, conscious intent to disclose, positive-negative (evaluation), and the relevance to the topic of discussion. The study results revealed five independent dimensions of self-disclosure:

- Intent to disclose
- Amount of disclosure including both frequency and duration
- The positive-negative nature of disclosure
- The honesty – accuracy of the disclosure
- The general depth – control of disclosure (p. 340-342).

In a later study, Wheeless (1976, p. 47-61), characterized the study of self-disclosure as a search for meaningful relationships. The results of his investigation of disclosure and relationships included the fact that self-disclosure and solidarity were positively related.

Biblical prisons and prisoners:

There are Israelites in the ancient times sited in the Old and New Testaments who demonstrated the impact of spirituality on their prison environment. The Mosaic Law established cities of refuge, places of protection (Numbers 35:22-28, NIV). The cities of refuge were for capitol offense cases and were provided to settle tensions of tribal law; retaliation and vengeance in which a blood relative was obligated to carry out vengeance; and civil law which follows specific codes of justice (NIV Study Bible, p. 241). The Mosaic Law did not include imprisonment which was not routinely practiced until the time of the Monarchy when prison confinement is said to have been a special part of the King's house (Nehemiah 3:25; Jeremiah 32:2, 3; 37:21).

According to Youngblood (p. 1030), prisons of the ancient world were crude and dehumanizing. There were several different types of prisons. There were prisons made from natural occurrences such as natural pits, and cave like dungeons. Prisoners are said to have been fed bread and water. As the main fare of the Israelites was bread, this may not have been cruel. Manmade structures for prisons were not common. Freeman (1996) writes that based on Eastern customs, state prisons were part of the dwelling, house of the chief of the executioners or some other prominent personage. Sometimes, the King's palace contained such designated areas (p. 45). During Paul's time, the Roman prisons were part of the government's headquarters (p. 1031). New Testament Jewish prisons were used to hold persons who were awaiting trial or execution, but they were not for punishment.

Daniel (NIV):

During a phase in the Battle of Babylon against Israel, Daniel, a teenager, was taken into Babylonian captivity. It does not appear that Daniel was in a prison at any time, but he was a captive. It was 605 BC when Daniel was taken to Babylon. He was in captivity for sixty years of his life, a lifer. Daniel's demeanor built a supportive climate with the official over him; this researcher believes there was trust built between the captor (chief official) and Daniel (the captive) (Daniel 1:18-19). Conflicts were handled peacefully; disclosure was obvious when Daniel explained how the King's fare would defile him. Daniel's spirituality was in his commitment to follow the Mosaic Law, and practices. He was controlled by his commitment, which was demonstrated throughout the book of Daniel.

Joseph (NIV):

Joseph was incarcerated in three different types of prisons:

- A pit
- The house of an official
- The King's palace (Genesis 37:23; 39:1, 2, 19-20).

Joseph was imprisoned for 14 years, and like Daniel, he was a teenager, 17, when first incarcerated. His imprisonment was about ¼ of the time spent by Daniel in captivity. Joseph, too, was led by his commitment to follow God. Joseph developed a supportive climate of trust with his jailer.

Paul (NIV)

In the New Testament, Paul is our chief inmate. Paul discusses the spiritual in 2 Corinthians 4:16-5:10. Paul explains that a spiritual change occurs during a person's present life time:

> Now it is God who has made us for this very purpose and has given us the Spirit as a deposit, guaranteeing what is to come (2 Corinthians 5:5).

This change to a living spiritual being requires a Christ-like Christian relationship. In Galatians, Paul expounds on living in freedom, a freedom to practice neighborly love without restrictions. According to Paul, the Spirit, true spirituality, will enable believers to transcend natural selfishness and to act generously (Galatians 5:13-16). Paul's theology of liberty, freedom from ritualistic law, is not free to sin, but free to live according to the Holy Spirit. As Gundry (1981) wrote, "Christians must lovingly help others…help another in present difficulties" (p. 252). This is supportive behavior. The Epistle of Romans, written by Paul, also discusses the result of the gift of the Holy Spirit which is peace, joy, and hope, in Chapter 5 these are aspects of spiritual fruit. It is this spirituality that provides the power to resist the control of sin, and choose spiritual control. Chapters 6-8 outline Christian Living.

Paul was imprisoned on several different occasions. His longest period of being in custody is four years (Youngblood, p. 954). Paul was imprisoned in Macedonia, in Philippi, in Caesarea, and in Rome. While imprisoned, Paul constantly preached Christ to the Governor. Although imprisoned, a church planting occurred in Macedonia (Youngblood, 953). While imprisoned, Paul demonstrated love in assisting Onesimus to gain spiritual freedom (Philemon).

In Philippi, while in chains, Paul demonstrated spiritual freedom as he and Silas sung hymns and psalms (Acts 16:25). In Rome, Paul was under house arrest and shackled to one of the soldiers responsible for guarding him. The guards operated in four hour shifts. A supportive communication climate was apparently generated as Paul was free to receive visitors and to discuss the gospel. Youngblood states, "Paul's restrictions should have produced an atmosphere that depresses communication, but the opposite occurred." Paul was free to correspond with friends in other parts of the Roman Empire. The Prison Epistles, letters Paul wrote during his imprisonment, are evidence of his being Spirit-controlled and exercising his spiritual freedom. The prison Epistles are Philippians, Colossians, Philemon, and Ephesians.

Methodology

The study is a descriptive investigation of the relationship between spiritual freedom and a positive communication climate within a restrictive environment. This is primarily a documentary study combined with limited field research. It is therefore a combination of objective study combined with a subjective, non-empirical approach.

Descriptive research is the study of existing conditions, situations, or relationships, in order to discover or establish norms of standards (Auer, 1959, p. 36).

The major aspects of a descriptive analysis are:
- A statement of the conditions or problems
- A working hypothesis or solution to a problem
- A research design which will identify conditions to be studied and a method of measuring the results (Auer, 24-52).

Simple observation is a tool of research. Normally this tool is used in situations in which the observer has no control over the behavior or situation in question, and therefore plays a passive and non-intrusive role in the research situation (Webb, et al, 1972, p. 112). This approach was used with professionals interviewed as part of the study. Reflective observation was used by the researcher in situations where specifics regarding participants, organizations/facilities, and locations were held in strict confidence or the facilities have been closed, therefore, only generalities can be reported.

The Study Design:

The study is a descriptive analysis combining the components of content analysis, and a communication audit. A content analysis looks at messages using methods which produce measurable units such as vocabulary used, key words, phrases or level of abstractions (Budd, thorp, and Donahew, 1967, P.2) Content analysis provides a systematic approach to analyze message content (p.2). The process of evaluation requires the categorizing/coding of message content. This will allow data to be scaled or grouped and quantified. A content analysis investigates the relationship of variables. The results of the study are based on the frequency of occurrence of key themes or key words (p.18-19). A communication audit is a procedure to assess the effectiveness of an organizational communication system according to a set of standards. (Goldhaber, 1974, p. 295).

As a descriptive analysis, the findings of this study, cannot be applied to organizations outside of the actual study group. However, the results may be used to evaluate current conditions in similar organizations.

The population of this study is persons serving life sentences and who have been imprisoned for at least twenty continuous years. The facility is a maximum security facility within the Michigan Department of Corrections system. The prison population is over 1000 inmates, and the lifer population was 26. The questionnaires were distributed by the office of the Warden, and nineteen (72%), responded. The responses were returned to the Warden's office and mailed to the investigator. Using concepts of Siang-Yang Tan regarding Spiritual disciplines (Siang, CD), the questionnaire was designed to describe the positive and negative aspects of the communication climate through self reports within the following four areas:

- Spiritual friends
- The willingness to self disclose to another
- The presence or absence of an attitude of trust
- The presence or absence of verbal conflict.

The questionnaire and cover letter are in the Appendix p. 77. 32% (6) of the respondents, selected randomly by the warden's office, were interviewed as a follow-up to self-reporting of spiritual freedom and spiritual control. Interview questions are provided in Appendix, p. 81.

Four professionals, clinical or licensed counselors, who have serviced and observed the incarcerated and who use Biblical constructs in their counseling were interviewed. It is believed that this group could evaluate the presence or absence of spirituality and could evaluate the communication climate. The questions asked of each professional are included in the Appendix, p. 83.

The researcher is the silent observer, reflecting on the communication climate and spirituality in three different prisons, two State facilities, and one Federal facility.

Table 3 - Respondents in the Study:

Classification	Group	Respondents	Percent of Group
Length of Incarceration	10 -20 years	3	17.6%
	21-30 years	13	64.7%
	31+ years	3	17.6%
Faith	Christianity	9	47.3%
	Islam	4	21.0%
	Other	4	21.0%
	None	1	5.2%
	No response	1	5.2%
Race/National Origin	Black	12	63.1%
	White	3	15.7%
	Other	4	21.0%
Age	30-40 Years old	2	10.5%
	41-60 years old	14	73.6%
	61 – 80+ years	3	15.7%

84% of the respondents, through self-assessment, are spiritual, regardless of faith or lack thereof. For persons incarcerated between ten and twenty continuous years, two of the three respondents claimed being spirit-controlled or having spirituality. In the group between 21 and 30 continuous years of incarceration, twelve of the thirteen respondents claimed being spirit-controlled or having spirituality, and in the group incarcerated for thirty-one plus continuous years, two of the three respondents claimed being spirit-controlled or having spirituality.

Table 4 - Self-Described Spirituality:

Length of Incarceration	Total Respondents	Number positive responses	Percent
10-20 years	3	2	.66
21-30 years	13	12	.92
31 + years	3	2	.66
Total	19	16	.84

Spiritual friends were determined from the responses of the respondents which pointed to a spiritual or Biblical content theme. The responses were calculated and compared to the group size. Table 6 has the listing of actual terms used by the respondents. Group 1, serving 10 – 21 years, used fourteen different words/phrases describing their spiritual friends. Within this small group, there was an average of five characteristics or themes to categorize persons or deities defined as friend(s) per inmate. This may indicate the need for more friend type relationships. In group 2, those serving 21 – 30 years, there were twenty-five words or phrases used to designate spiritual friends; on an average of two per respondent, the relationships tend to be smaller in the larger grouping. In group 3, those serving thirty-one plus years, there were thirteen different words/themes to express the concept of a spiritual friend. The average for this small group was four different themes per person. It is noted that this group includes the oldest inmates as well as those serving the longest time. The need for spiritual friends regresses to earlier times.

Table 5 – Themes for Spiritual Friends:

Group	Total Respondents	Number of Thematic Designations	Average Number
I (10-20 years)	3	15	5
II (21 – 30)	13	25	2
III (31 +)	3	13	4
Total	19	53 2.8	

Table 6 – Spiritual Designations/Themes of Friends

Group	God Related Themes	Scripture Related Themes
I	Lord	Lord is my Light
	Awesome	No worry
	Love	Accepting
	Dying on the Cross	Fellowship
	Wisdom	
	Faithful	
	Amazing	
	Merciful	
	Trusting	
II	Spirit	Freedom
	Almighty	Never Forsaken
	Love	God so loved
	Lord	He loves me
	Forgiver	Spirit of God in me
	Faithful	There is no condemnation
	Supreme	Friend
	Trusting	No worry
	Safe	Respect

Table 6a – Spiritual Designations/Themes of Friends:

Group	God Related Themes	Scripture Related Themes
II	Father Jesus Merciful Eternal	
III	Love (3)*[1] Spirit Almighty Forgiver	God's Spirit is in me No life taken Death (2)* Service Daily Life Jesus is with us

    To further describe the spiritual friends in relation to the communication events, respondents were asked to report how they show the value of a person, whom do they allow into their communication space and to whom do they communicate with daily. The themes designating friends parallel the behavior demonstrated in the interpersonal communication events.

---

[1] * indicates theme used this number of times.

Table 7 – Behavior Designating Spiritual Friends:

Group	Behavior Showing Value	Persons allowed into Personal Space	Those having Daily Communication with
I	My words My moral behavior Treating as God's child	God Truth	Myself Jesus Family Others
II	Reciprocal treatment Forgiveness Witness of Christ Kindness Commitment	God Friends No one Family	God Friends Jesus Pastor Others
III	Help them Give them second chances My behavior	Others Love Peace	God Others Myself

Questions relating to:

- Seeking information
- Receiving honest answers
- Disagreeing freely
- Having friendly relationships
- Having a positive or negative attitude toward administration
- Discussing personal problems
- Assessing information sources were used to describe the inmate's assessment of a trusting environment.

Table 8 Described Trusting Climate:

Variables of Trust	Group	Responses
Seek opinion of others	I	God
		Family
		Friends
		Other
	II	God
		Chaplain
		Closest Friends
		My Lord
		Pastor
		Others

Table 8a Trusting Climate

Variables of Trust	Group	Responses
Seek opinion of others	III	Inner thoughts
		Other
Deemed honest	I	Attorney
		Warden
	II	Chaplain
		Christ
		Some Staff
	III	No response
Free to indicate disagreement	I	Each other
	II	Chaplain
		Each other
		Anyone
	III	Staff
		Others
Disclosing wrongs	I	God
		My Family

Table 8b Trust Climates

Variables of Trust	Group	Responses
Disclosing Wrongs	I	Myself
	II	God
		Closest Friends
		Myself
		Chaplain
		Wife
		Sister
		No one
	III	Christ
		Friends
		No one
Friendly Relationships	I	God
		Family Members
	II	God
		Family
		Jesus Christ
		My Lord
		Most People
		Others

Table 8c - Trust Climate

Variables of Trust	Group	Responses
Friendly Relationships	III	God
		Medical Staff
		Certain Staff
Feelings toward Administration	I	Undecided
		OK
		Good
	II	Positive
		Good
		Mixed
		Doubtful
		Fair
		Up & down
		Godly
		Bad
	III	Trusting
		Mixed
		Good
Discussion of Personal Problems	I	Christ
		No one

Table 8d - Trust Climate:

Variables of Trust	Group	Responses
Discussion of Personal Problems	II	Chaplain
		Jesus Christ
		Mother
		God
		Wife
		Close Friends
		Pastor
		Family
	III	Anyone
		God
		My friends
Source of trustworthy Information	I	God
		Family
	II	Family
		The Bible
		The Lord
		Wife
		God

Table 8e - Trust Climate

Variables of Trust	Group	Responses
Trustworthy information	II	Pastor
		Sister
	III	Home
		The Bible
		My Family
Who has confidence in me?	I	Family
		My Children
		My mother
	II	Family
		People
		Membership
		Some Friends
		The Lord
		Wife
		Son
		Grandmother
		Mentor

Table 8f - Trust Climate

Variables of Trust	Group	Responses
Who has Confidence in me?	III	Christ
		Staff
		Prisoners
No Fear of Disagreeing	I	Other inmates
		Anyone
		The wrong
	II	Authority
		Anything
		Any member
		The Lord
		No one
		Mentor
		Those who are wrong
	III	Other Prisoners
		Staff
		Mankind

Disclosure was described through the answers to questions related to sharing personal information, intimacy of topics discussed, and the ability to share an emotional release without shame.

Table 9 - Disclosure

Variable	Group	Responses
With whom do I have emotional release with no shame?	I	Listeners
		My children
	II	Mother
		Myself
		My people
		No one
		Wife
		Friends
		God
		Family
		Christ
		Jesus
	III	Others
		Christ
		Doctor
		Psychiatrist

Table 9a - Disclosure

Variables	Group	Responses
With whom do I share personal information?	I	Anyone
		Family
		Those I trust
	II	Others
		Close Friends (2)*
		Mother
		Case manager
		Friends
		Myself
		Mentor
		God
	III	God
		Medical Staff
		Nobody

Table 9b - Disclosure

Variables	Group	Responses
I do not share this information	I	What others tell me
		My childhood
		My Family
	II	About another person (2)*
		Personal things
		Inner self
	III	Family
		Myself and God
		My case
		Myself
Topics not discussed	I	Health
		Appeal
	II	God
		Christ
		Getting out
		Prison reform
		Me
		Lord
		Medical
		Freedom
		Life
		God's will/Purpose

    The presence and absence of conflict was described by the nature of verbal conflict, elapsed time since the last verbal conflict, and how the conflicts were resolved. Verbal conflict was assessed because verbal differences often precede other forms of conflicts. Verbal issues affect the communication environment. Table 10 describes the last variable involved in describing the communication climate.

Table 10 - Verbal Conflict

Variables	Group	Responses
Subject of conflict	I	Disrespect
		Money
		My Case
	II	Cleanliness
		Racial slurs
		Faith in God
		Money
		Playing with others
		The devil
		Don't know
		Getting support
		Freedom
	III	God
		Staff stealing from me
		Money

Table 10a - Conflict

Variables	Group	Responses
Methods Resolving Conflicts	I	Fighting
		Letting go
	II	Debate
		Discussion
		Talking
		Walking away
		Receiving a ticket
		Through an inmate
		Through family members
	III	Through a friend
		Filing a grievance
		Talking it over
Date of Last Conflict (Date of the questionnaire 8/2012	I	09/2011
		08/2012
		01/2006
	II	08/2012
		08/2012
		06/2012

Table 10b - Conflicts

Variables	Group	Responses
Date of Last verbal conflict	II	03/2012
		09/2007
	III	07/2012
		08/2012
With Whom was the Verbal Conflict	I	Another inmate
		My family
		The Court
	II	A prisoner
		Staff
		People
		Wife
		Fellow inmate
		Myself
		Officer
		Inmate
		Female I know
	III	Inmate
		Corrections Officer

Table 10c - Conflicts

Variables	Group	Responses
Nature of the Conflict	I	Disrespecting me
		Can't say
		Failure to send secure package
	II	Miscommunication
		Existence of God
		Misunderstanding
		"N" and "B" words
		Sexual misconduct
		Kids
		Gambling debt
		Living life right
	III	Show me God
		Need love
		Shake down by Correctional Officer

The content analysis of the descriptive themes and words which describe the communication climate were placed into general categories. In the assessment of spiritual friends, three general categories were identified:

    Category 1.   God/Jesus/Lord

    Category 2.   Love

    Category 3.   Faithfulness/trust

Category 1 was used 15 times to distinguish spiritual friends. Category 2 was used 13 times, and category 3 was used 6 times. Other descriptives did not indicate patterns.

The major relational behavior characteristics were respect and kindness. The major relationships with which the inmates had daily communications were of a spiritual nature, God/Jesus, and clergy/chaplain. Friends exceeded the category of family for daily communications. This may be a result of the incarceration. Another theme was self communication. The themes of intimacy and trust were placed in five major categories:

- Family
- Christ/God/Lord
- Friends
- Chaplain/Pastor
- Self.

There was not a consistent theme in the area of sharing information, but Friends, God, and Family were indicated more than once. Sharing through emotional release was in two main areas, family and God/Christ. Information not shared indicates that intimacy regarding self and family is protected. The two themes discussed the most were God/Religion and Release.

In the area of verbal conflicts, the length of time since the last conflict ranged from 0 months to 72 months. The shorter the length of incarceration, the shorter the time between verbal conflicts. The most consistent themes of the conflict were money and faith. Conflicts were primarily resolved through communication techniques or avoidance. The conflicts normally were between other inmates or with staff.

Inmate Interviews:

Inmate interviewees were selected by the Warden's office. The interviewers were the Researcher and an assistant, a religious volunteer who participates in prison ministry. Each interview was tape recorded for purposes of security and integrity of the correctional system, and to provide a record, if requested, to the Warden's office. The tape also assisted with the summarizing of the information received from the interviews. The interviews were conducted in the Staff conference room of the correctional facility on October 12, 2012.

John has served one year of his life sentence. He has been converted, and his religion is Baptist. His conversion occurred prior to his incarceration. He professed being indwelled with the Holy Spirit, and he stated he was spiritually free. When asked to describe his current freedoms as an inmate, he said, "I know some things better. I don't have to give up. My body is locked up, but my mind is free. I am not scared to dream. I am loved by myself, by God, and by others." John was asked to describe his spiritual freedoms as an inmate. His response, "I do know God loves me, Jesus loves me; my actions describe what I say; what I do matters to God. This reflects my actions." He stated he spends 90% of the day in conversation with others. When asked with whom he communicates the most, John said, "My roommate, a brother down the hall." He said, "I try not to be judgmental in my conversation. I am more mature; I have something to live for, and I have not given up. My communication is positive. I give others my testimony, and I seek to help them understand; they are 18, 19, and 20 years old." John prays three times a day, and he reads his Bible twice a day. His answer to the question, are you currently content, was no and yes. "I was rescued, preserved for a purpose. I was loved enough to be saved. This is my yes contentment. My no is because I am away from family, but I am mentally and physically content."

Thomas has been incarcerated for twenty years. He said he has not been converted, and he described his faith as that of a naturist. When asked had he been indwelled with the Holy Spirit, he replied yes. When asked if he was spiritually free, his response was yes. In describing his current inmate freedoms, Thomas said, "I am mentally free, I can express myself intellectually; I am not holding back on my mind; I have the ability to smile. I accept my pains; I know I hurt my children, my mother, and my grandmother in coming to prison. I express my beliefs to a higher self." When asked if he had spiritual freedom as an inmate, his answer was, "I have no other freedoms." Thomas said he spends about three hours of his 10 hour day in communication. He communicates most with his cell mate. He prays three times a day and in between. He said, "I talk to a higher self. I read my Bible twice a day; I read the Koran twice a day." His response to being content was an emphatic no.

Lee has been continuously incarcerated for twenty-three years. He was converted and is of the Baptist faith. He stated he was not incarcerated at the time of his conversion. His response to have you been indwelled with the Holy Spirit was yes. He answered affirmatively to being spiritually free. He described his inmate freedoms as "My mind is free; my conscience is free; the demons are gone. I have no burdens." Lee's response when asked to describe your spiritual freedoms was, "Hope and happiness…Life is what it means to live as a man now….before I was living in sin, now I understand and have a new focus. I am not living in a dark area." Lee said he spends 90% of his time in conversation with others, and he communicates most with his 'bunkie'; because I am always locked in with him. There is a friend I grew up with, and I try to talk with him as much as I can. I call my mother a lot." His prayer time is always before he goes to bed. "I don't read my bible often enough; I read more in law. I am partly content, part because I am locked-up. I just need to live life fully in Christ. I have not reached that yet. I am still fighting to get out."

    Tyrone has been continuously incarcerated for forty-two years. He stated he has never been converted. He said, "I do not know if I have been indwelled by the Holy Spirit." When asked if he was spiritually free, Tyrone said yes. Tyrone described his inmate freedoms in an ironic manner. He said his freedom came from "the time I did here. I used to have hope and faith. My mother said, 'Pray,' and I didn't know how. I don't care. My light at the end of my tunnel is dim. I didn't kill anyone. I was wrong; why is my punishment so severe?" When asked if he could describe his inmate spiritual freedoms. Tyrone's response was I do not know my spiritual freedoms, but I would like to know. Tyrone spends 2/3 of his time in conversation with others. The convicts are those with whom he communicates most. When asked how often he prayed during the day, his response was, "I don't". When asked how often he read his Bible during a day, he answered, "I think about quotes in the Bible, and references with others everyday. Psalm 23 is the Psalm my grandmother always read." When asked about contentment, Tyrone said no because of incarceration.

    Tom has been continuously incarcerated for twenty-seven years. He stated he has not been converted, but he would like to be. He said he has not been indwelled with the Holy Spirit, and he is not spiritually free. In describing his freedom as an inmate, his answer was I am free in mind. Tom works as a tutor, so most of his day is in conversation with others. Coworkers are the persons with whom he communicates the most. He never prays, but he reads his Bible several hours a day. He stated he is not content.

Richard has been incarcerated for thirty-seven years. He was converted to the Muslim faith. He stated he was not incarcerated at the time of his conversion. He stated he was indwelled with the Holy Spirit, and he is spiritually free. In describing his freedoms as an inmate, he stated he was in tune with spiritual aspects as well as carnal aspects. He is attempting to be more in tune with the spiritual. His spiritual freedoms were described as not being concerned with carnal things, because they are temporary. Richard spends 80% of his day in conversation with others. The persons with whom he communicates the most are people in religion. He stated he prays throughout the day and he reads his Bible daily along with his prayers. He stated he was currently content.

Professional Interviews:

Interviews of professional clinicians working in the area of corrections were conducted to provide reliability and validity to the self-reported assessments of the inmates. Silent observations of the researcher were another tool for validity and reliability.

Clinical Psychologist, Dr. Y. interviewed October 20, 2012, Detroit, Michigan:

Dr. Y, now retired, provided counseling to inmates and parolees in the Federal system for thirty years. She stated that during the last twenty years of her practice, she used Christian Theology in the counseling process. She stated she serviced persons after incarceration, and many had served up to thirty years. Dr. Y. said she had the opportunity to observe inmates in none counseling/teaching situations. As a psychologist, her services included assessment of mental states. She stated she observed language used which indicated spirituality and being spirit-controlled. The example given was that of a "hit man" who became a believer, became one who believed in good and evil, and was able to control his beliefs. Language usage was in phrases such as "the battle is the Lord's." Those who were Christians readily talked about Christ. Those who were not spiritual were seeking to "make good who they were."

Licensed Counselor and Retired Chaplain, Reverend Dr. Billy Ray Thompson, Sr., Interviewed October 29, 2012, Detroit, Michigan:

The Reverend Dr. Thompson is a licensed Counselor who has a Doctor of Ministry Degree. He worked as an institutional Chaplain within the State of Michigan's Correction Department. Dr. Thompson retired from chaplaincy after eighteen years of service. He has provided counseling, since 2005, as an independent contractor. Dr. Thompson is an ex-offender. He is writing a book, describing his life from the penitentiary to the pulpit. He reported that he used and uses Christian Theology in the counseling process. He stated he dealt with thirteen different beliefs as a Chaplain, and he was able on a daily basis to observe inmates in non-counseling/teaching environments. He stated he was able to observe behavior which would indicate spirituality. He stated language demonstrating spirituality was observed. Along with uplifting activities, non-spirituality was noted among those with homosexuality issues, and issues of racism. He stated groups formed on spirituality were observed more among religious groups, and Muslims could be observed in prayer. He stated Christian groups met for Bible study, and although it was against the rules, inmates would pool resources to aid newcomers. This action was to prevent the newcomer from becoming prey. In personal groups, there was testimony of disclosure of substance abuse, and of sex offenders. He stated that outside of group situations, "people knew the background of the people." The inmate population knew inmate backgrounds before the officers on duty. Dr. Thompson stated that trust normally followed the general rule of the institution. Prisoners do not trust staff. Inmates can't become overly familiar with staff. He stated, "Christians who had Christ in their lives demonstrated genuine trust." He saw brotherhood develop. He did not observe verbal conflicts. He stated fellowship developed across racial lines.

Certified Biblical Counselor, Missionary Christina Dixon Interviewed October 29, 2012, Detroit, Michigan:

Missionary Christina Dixon is an ordained Home Missionary and a certified Biblical Counselor. She has served the incarcerated for over ten years by providing Christian Bible classes and relationship education. Missionary Dixon integrates Biblical Theology in her teaching and training. She indicated she had never observed inmates in a non-counseling/teaching environment. 90% of her observations were in classroom settings and worship components. She has observed spirituality in such actions as prayer and worship. She stated she heard the use of spiritual language such as quoting scriptures. The environment was not restrictive and open relationships were seen. She observed the witnessing of one's faith as well as statements of disclosures regarding topics such as infidelity, remorse over being in an inappropriate relationship with minors, and having poor parenting practices. These disclosures in some situations resulted in seeking forgiveness. Trust was observed in inmates' willingness to hear counsel and receive correction. There was a willingness among the inmates to provide explanation to those who appeared not to understand an issue. She noted that among those she believed to be less spiritual, there were more verbal disagreements. Fellowship was observed in observing language of encouragement, comfort, and affirmation to those showing real feelings. These were 'truth-telling,' after firm non-hostile confrontation. She stated she observed inmates who had a commitment to Christ; desire to demonstrate their commitment to their loved ones and family members who were not incarcerated.

<u>Counselor, Reverend Audry Turner, Interviewed October 29, 2012, Detroit, Michigan:</u>

Rev. Turner has a Masters in Pastoral Counseling and is completing a Doctorate of Divinity in Pastoral Counseling. Rev. Turner is a counselor in the judicial system counseling ex-offenders and connecting them with mentors. Her services to ex-offenders include Bible Study, preaching, and performing weddings. She has provided services to ex-offenders for over ten years. She has observed offenders in non-counseling situations, and found them to be guarded, depressed, and acting OK but are not OK. Their talk was about regrets or remorse and getting through prison life. Rev. Turner stated she never saw spirituality outside of the worship service. She did not observe spirituality during visitations. She stated that in the beginning of their time of incarceration, their conversation is bitter; they are seventeen when they go in but are 25 or 40 when in the last years of incarceration. Rev. Turner stated she integrates Theology into her counseling only if the inmate gives an in-road to the approach. Her approach is to help them apply spiritual insight. She never heard an inmate confess their faith or make disclosures. She reported that inmates form alliances, but her experience is they don't know who to trust, except to meet personal needs; they operate to receive money or sexual favors. She never heard verbal conflicts, and fellowships were only in sports or with bunkies. She stated she worked in the past with a program, Transition of Prisoners. She noted spirituality from participants who were practicing Christianity. These persons were in a program, and their selection was to enable them to continue their relationship with Christ.

Field Study Results and Analysis

The field results through descriptive analysis will compare the variables of spiritual freedom with the variables of positive interpersonal interaction within the communication climate. The communication climate variables are spiritual friends, self disclosure, attitude of trust, and amount of verbal conflict. Spiritual freedom is being spiritually controlled by the fruit of the Spirit: love, joy, peace, longsuffering, kindness, goodness, faith, meekness, and self-control.

Evidence of Spiritual Freedom:

Do words used by the respondents to describe components of spiritual friends describe the fruit of the spirit? The following words were used multiple times to describe spiritual friends: love, faithful, steadfast, trusting, safe, forgiving, merciful, service, respect, and kindness. These words match the words or biblical definitions of the fruit of the Spirit. The clinical psychologist, Dr. Y, and Biblical Counselor, Missionary Dixon, in their observations of behavior and/or speech of inmates, indicated a positive interaction between the variables of spiritual fruit and the communication climate. Spiritual friends were designated as God, Jesus, the Holy Spirit, a Higher Power, and persons not physically in their environment. This indicates the use of prayer as a means of communicating with spiritual friends, and correlates with the fact that respondents regularly have daily prayer. Again these are indications of being spiritually free. Prayer was viewed as a mechanism for controlling the physical environment according to the counselors interviewed.

The variable of trust was described by the inmates in four main categories: Spiritual friends, Spiritual representatives (Chaplain/Pastor), Family, and a general Other category. A main category of trust was in a religious direction and was described as trust in God, My Lord, Christ, and the Bible. These were repeated descriptors. This variable would match the faith fruit in the Fruit of the Spirit. This would indicate an environment where self-disclosure would be more likely to occur.

Disclosure, an indication of a positive interpersonal communication climate appears closely related to the spiritual fruit of love, peace, kindness, and goodness. Disclosure was described as sharing personal self-information and achieving emotional release, i.e. crying without shame. Disclosure was described to have occurred on several levels: Spiritual friends, Spiritual Representatives, Family, and Others. Although the environment apparently gave freedom to disclose, the inmates guarded the information which they chose to share. Missionary Dixon reported that when in small groups, disclosure was more intimate, including topics of infidelity, and sexual misconduct. The topics most discussed within general communications involved their spiritual status including such topics as God, Christ, The Lord, God's Will, and God's purpose. This would indicate being Spirit-controlled in selecting topics for discussion.

Absence of verbal conflict was used as an indicator of the fruit of peace, to describe interpersonal communication during times of troubles. The rate of verbal conflicts was approximately one per month; however, the methods of resolution indicated being spiritually free to resolve through communication or to walk away from the issue; only one instance ended in a physical altercation, as reported. Although not a consistent pattern, the longest time without a verbal conflict was 72 months (6 years). There is evidence of a climate conducive to resolving problems peacefully.

Reliability of Spiritual Freedom Concepts:

The random inmate interviews described personal freedom and spiritual freedom. The interviewees, who recognized themselves as having been converted and indwelled with the Holy Spirit, had merged their personal freedoms and spiritual freedoms, and the ability to discriminate between the two was minimal. Among the interviewees who had not been converted, they found no spiritual freedoms nor indicated spiritual control. They did not pray; however they did read Scriptures. This adds to the validity of being spiritual, and the impact that spirituality has on the communication climate. Because of the small number in the sample, this result is only applicable to those interviewed. The variable of contentment was based on Paul's statement, "...For I have learned to be content... I know what it is to be in need, and I know what it is to have plenty. I have learned the secret of being content in any and every situation, whether well fed or hungry, whether living in plenty or in want" (Philippians 4: 11-12, NIV). The inmates' contentment was based on their physical state, separated from loved ones, and not just on their spiritual state or inner peace.

Conclusions and Implications

Hypothesis #1:

      A high degree of spiritual freedom will produce a positive communication climate. There is a general description of a positive interpersonal communication tone among the lifers who identified themselves as being spiritually controlled.

Hypothesis #2:

      Spirituality is exhibited through spiritual behaviors. Spiritual behaviors are having a character that exhibits the Fruit of the Spirit: love, joy, peace, longsuffering, goodness, faith, meekness, and self-control. Based on the self-reports, these characteristics were present in 84% of the respondents, and the range was 66% - 92% of the target groups.

Hypothesis #3:

      Spirituality will result in exhibited behavior which identifies positive relationships with spiritual friends. Spiritual friends were noted in each grouping of the incarcerated. The categories of spiritual friends described the spiritual environment and paralleled the characteristics of spirituality.

Hypothesis #4:

      Spirituality will be exhibited in the willingness to self-disclose to another. The description of disclosure indicates that those who are spiritual have relationships which provide avenues for disclosure and emotional release.

Hypothesis #5:

      Spirituality will provide behavior which demonstrates an attitude of trust. The descriptions indicated that those who are Spirit-controlled have objects of trust which include staff other than the Chaplain. This is contrary to the observations and experiences of Rev. Turner.

Hypothesis #6:

Spirituality will provide behavior which is void of verbal conflict. The descriptions of this variable did not support the hypothesis. The descriptors did support that spirituality provides an environment to resolve conflict through peaceful means.

Implications:

Spirituality was shown to have a positive impact on the interpersonal communication climate of those serving life sentences. The use of a descriptive analysis was limiting, only describing the target population, and not having any predictive value nor establishing a causal relationship. The results indicate there is value in activities which provide a spiritual approach to meet the emotional, mental, and spiritual needs of the inmates. The results support the concept that spiritual freedoms are not based on being physically free.

The results support that there are positive benefits to providing faith-based programs particularly for newcomers as well as long-timers.

The areas of future study should include:

A. What degree of spirituality is necessary to affect contentment among those serving life sentences?

B. What degree of contentment is possible among lifers who are void of spirituality?

C. Does the spirituality of staff have a positive or negative impact on interpersonal relationships of the long-term incarcerated?

D. Is there a causal relationship between a lifer being spirit-controlled and the characteristics of his/her interpersonal communications?

This study has attempted to explore and to describe the communication climate of those incarcerated for life and their exercise of spiritual freedoms.

Appendices

- Approval Letter of the Study
- Inmate Questionnaire (blank)
- Interview Questionnaire for Inmates
- Questions for Professional Counselors

STATE OF MICHIGAN
DEPARTMENT OF CORRECTIONS
LANSING

RICK SNYDER
GOVERNOR

DAN HEYNS
DIRECTOR

July 23, 2012

Dear Dr. Jackson:

We have reviewed the documentation submitted for your proposed research on the, "Spiritual Freedom" of those incarcerated with life sentences (25 years or more). Based on this documentation, we are hereby notifying you that your study will be approved as required by PD 01.04.120 provided that you send us a letter acknowledging the following conditions. A copy of this letter must accompany all publications resulting from this study.

- Please point-out in this letter that your approval to proceed should not be interpreted as an endorsement by the Michigan Department of Corrections of your methodology or findings;
- This research project is a qualitative study of the relationships between levels of spiritual freedom and communication climates within prison environments;
- The sample is small and the data is self-reported, thus results are not applicable beyond the cases in the sample;
- This research will report content analysis of offenders' levels of spiritual freedom and amounts of positive or negative attitudes within prison environments;
- Subject participation is strictly voluntary. Potential study subjects will be advised that no benefit or negative consequences will accrue to them from their decision whether or not to participate in the surveys or interviews;
- All data from this study will be kept strictly confidential and no identifying information or information which could lead to discovery of the identity of the study participants will be included in any report or other presentation of the study;
- Data collected for this study will not be accessible to anyone other than the researchers and will be retained in a location which is physically secure (paper records) or electronically secure (magnetic tapes or computer records);
- No MDOC resources (including staff time, MDOC equipment, etc.) will be used for this study;
- And, Research's approval is only for the research content of this study. Final operational approval to proceed must be obtained from warden(s) of the facilities(s) involved based on their professional judgment as to the ability of their staff to accommodate your requests without disrupting normal facility operations. Wardens will also determine which inmates may complete questionnaires, which inmates may be interviewed, locations for these interviews, and if tape recorders and cassettes may be brought into their facilities.

Upon receipt of your letter accepting these conditions, we will issue a final letter of approval. You must provide a copy of this approval letter upon request as documentation of Research's approval. You should also retain signed copies of participants' consent forms in your records so that they may be furnished upon request.

If you have any questions, or if we can be of any further assistance, please let me know.

Sincerely,

Kenneth J. Bush, Departmental Specialist
Risk/Classification and Program Evaluation Section
Office of Research and Planning

cc: Stephen DeBor, Administrator, Office of Research and Planning
R. Douglas Kosinski, Manager, Program Evaluation Section
Norma Killough, Departmental Specialist, Correctional Facilities Administration

July 25, 2012

Mr. Kenneth J. Bush, Departmental Specialist
Risk/Classification and Program Evaluation Section
Office of Research and Planning
Department of Corrections, State of Michigan
P.O. Box 30003
Lansing, Michigan 48909

Dear Mr. Bush:

In accordance with the stipulations in your tentative approval letter of July 23, 2012 for my proposed research, I acknowledge and accept the following conditions.

- The approval to proceed with the study will not be interpreted as an endorsement by the Michigan Department of Corrections of my methodology or findings.
- This is a qualitative rather than quantitative study of the relationships between levels of spiritual freedom and communicative climates within prison environments.
- The research sample is small and the data is self-reported, thus the results cannot be applied beyond the cases in the sample;
- The research will report content analysis of offenders levels of spiritual freedom and amounts of positive or negative attitudes within the prison environment(s).
- Subject participation is strictly voluntary.
- Potential study subjects will be advised that no benefit or negative consequences will accrue to them from their decision whether or not participate in the surveys or interviews.
- All data from this study will be kept strictly confidential and no identifying information or information which could lead to discovery of the identity of the study participants will be included in any report or other presentation of the study.
- Data collected for the study will not be accessible to anyone other than the researchers and paper records will be retained in a locked file, and electronic data will be maintained on a flesh drive maintained in a secured locked container.
- No MDOC resources (staff time, equipment) will be used for this study.
- The research approval is for study content.
- Operational approval is to be obtained the facilities, wardens. The involvement of the facility is based on the warden's professional judgment as to their staff being able to accommodate my requests without disrupting normal facility operations.
- The warden(s) will determine which inmates may complete questionnaires, and which inmates may be interviewed, and if tape recorders and cassettes may be bought into their facilities.

It is requested that warden(s) will provide the researcher the criteria used in selecting participants. This effects the random selection, within a specific classification, process.

Thank you for your assistance in this research project. A hard copy of this letter is being mailed via US mail, along with a hard copy of the letter of July 23, 2012, emailed to me.

Sincerely,

Brenda Simuel Jackson, PH.D
Jacksonville Theological Seminary Student
Researcher

Cc: Dr. James H. Vick II, Academic Dean. Jacksonville Theological Seminary
JTSjax@jts.edu

SURVEY

Section I: Demographics
Check only one (1) response for each question.

1. I have been continuously incarcerated:

   __ 10-20 years   __ 21-30 years   __ 31 or more years

2. What is your age?

   __ 30-40 years   __ 41-60 years   __ 61-80 plus years

3. What is your faith?
   __ Buddhism   __ Christianity   __ Hinduism
   __ Islam   __ Judaism   __ Other   __ None

4. What is your race, national origin, or color?
   __ Black   __ Hispanic   __ Native Born
   __ Oriental   __ White   __ Other

Section II: Personal assessment of being Spirit controlled or having Spirituality:

1.	I am more than a physical being.	True	False
2.	I have an active prayer life.	True	False
3.	I provide service to those in need.	True	False
4.	I forgive those who mistreat me.	True	False
5.	I exercise self-control over my behavior and my thoughts.	True	False
6.	I love and I am loved.	True	False
7.	I am worthy of respect and I give respect	True	False
8.	I am humble to God.	True	False
9.	I submit to God and obey Him.	True	False

10. I can be trusted.	True	False
11. I do not let anger control me.	True	False
12. I am gentle and kind spirited.	True	False
13. I have been forgiven my sins.	True	False
14. I am patient.	True	False
15. I have learned how to wait.	True	False
16. I am honest in my speech and my actions.	True	False

Section III: Assessment of Spiritual Friendships:

Please respond (print response) to each question as requested by the question.

1. <u>In one sentence</u>, describe how you know God is tuned into your situation.
2. If you had <u>one word or image</u> to describe God right now, what would it be?
3. If Christ were sitting next to you, what would be the <u>topic</u> of your conversation?
4. In your current situation, in <u>one to three words</u>, describe the goodness of God.
5. <u>Complete this sentence</u>. Since I face never being released from prison, and since God is in control of everything, my attitude toward God is _____.
6. Scripture helps me to deal with my circumstances. (Circle one)

    True   False

7. <u>List</u> the scripture passages that help you the most.
8. From the previously listed scriptures, which passage has strengthened your relationship with God?
9. It helps me to know that Christ suffered for me. (Circle one)

    True   False

10. Describe how is life different for you when you see God as your Father and Christ as your Friend?
11. **(Complete this sentence)** I demonstrate how I value a person by _____.
12. **(Fill in the blank)** I allow _____ into my personal space.
13. **(Fill in the blank)** I communicate with _____ daily.

Section IV: Assessment of attitude of trust: Please fill in the blanks.
1. I seek the opinion of _____ before making my decision.
   _{Position}
2. _____ is honest with the inmates.
3. Inmates are free to disagree with _____.
4. I tell _____ when things go wrong.
5. I have a friendly relationship with _____.
6. I have _____ feelings toward administration.
7. I can discuss personal problems with _____.
8. Information I receive from _____ is trustworthy.
9. _____ has confidence in me.
10. I have no fear in disagreeing with _____.

Section V: Disclosure: Fill in the blank
1. I share personal information about myself with _____.
2. I am able to achieve emotional release (tears, no shame), when communicating with _____.
3. I do not share information about _____.
4. The topic I discuss most is _____.

Section VI: Assessment of verbal conflict: Fill in the blank

1. The last verbal conflict I had was about _____.
2. My last verbal conflict happened in - Month _____ Year_____
3. I resolve my conflicts by _____
4. My verbal conflicts were with _____
   _{Position}

5. <u>Describe</u> your last verbal conflict.

Interview Document

Spiritual Freedom with the Communication Climate

Interviewer: _____

Date: _____

Time: _____

Introduction: I am _____. I am assisting in conducting a study of spiritual freedom among the incarcerated, particularly, inmates serving life sentences. The information gathered from this interview is confidential, and you will not be identified as a participant in the study. Your participation is voluntary. There are no special benefits in participating or not participating in this study. Are you willing to proceed with the interview?

Questions:
1. How long have you been continuously incarcerated?
2. What name shall I call you?
3. Have you been converted?   Yes   No
4. If 3 is yes, what religion?
5. Were you incarcerated at the time of your conversion? Yes   No
6. If 5 is yes, how long had you been incarcerated before your conversion?
7. Have you been indwelled with the Holy Spirit?
   Yes   No   If no, end the interview; if yes go to #8
8. Are you spiritually free?   Yes   No
9. Describe your current freedoms as an inmate:

10. Describe your spiritual freedoms as an inmate:

11. What percent of the day do you spend in conversation with others?

12. Who are the persons with whom you communicate the most?

13. How often do you pray during a day?

14. How often do you read your Bible during a day?

15. Are you currently content?   Yes   No

Signature of the Interviewer: _____

Questions for Professional Interviews

1. Name?
2. Educational attainment?
3. Are you a trained psychologist or counselor? How much experience do you have as a professional counselor?
4. Do you integrate Christian Theology into your counseling?
5. Have you provided service to the imprisoned/incarcerated?
6. Have you serviced inmates serving 10 or more continuous years behind bars?
7. What services did you provide these inmates?
8. Have you had the opportunity to observe the behavior of these inmates in non-counseling/teaching situations?
9. In your observation did you notice behavior which would indicate spirituality, such as prayer, bible reading, other areas of worship?
10. Did you observe language usage that would indicate spirituality, such as appealing to a Higher authority, or quoting scripture?
11. Did you hear any profess faith or witness about their faith?
12. Did you observe personal disclosure, openness in interpersonal communication among those who appeared spiritual?
13. If #12 is yes, How would you describe the disclosure?
14. Did you observe evidence of trust or confidence among those who appear spiritual? Describe your observations.
15. Did you observe any verbal conflicts involving those who appear to be spiritual?
16. How would you fellowship among those who appear spiritual?

References

Aday, R.H. (2003). *Aging Prisoners, Crisis in American Corrections.* Westport: Praeger.

Archer, G.R. (1994). *A Survey of the Old Testament*. Chicago: Moody Press.

Auer, J.J. (1959). *An Introduction To Research In Speech*. New York: Harper & Row Publishers.

Barker, K. (Gen. Ed.). (1985). *The NIV Study Bible, New International Version.* Grand Rapids, Michigan: Zondervan Bible Publishers.

Berlo, D.K. (1960). *The Process of Communication.* New York: Holt, Rinehart, and Winston.

Bruce, F.T. (1977). *Paul Apostle of the Heart Set Free.* Grand Rapids, Michigan: William B. Eerdmans Publishing Co.

Budd, R.W., Thorp, R.K., Donahew, L. (1967). *Content Analysis of Communications.* New York: MacMillan.

Casarjean, R. (1996). *House of Healing – A Prisoner's Guide To Inner Power and Freedom.* USA: Lionheart Press.

Clinton, T. & Straub, J. (2010). *God Attachments.* New York: Howard Books.

Collins, G.R. (2001). *The Biblical Basis of Christian Counseling for People Helpers.* USA: NavPress.

Daniels, D. et. al. (1995). *The African Cultural Heritage Topical Bible KJV.* USA: Pneuma Life Publishing.

Dow, C.W. (Ed.). (1961). *An Introduction to Graduate Study in Speech and Theatre.* East Lansing, Michigan: Michigan University Press.

Ehrlich, S.D. (2011). Spirituality. University of Maryland Medical Center. Retrieved July 27, 2012 on the World Wide Web: http://www.umm.edu/Articles/Spirituality-00360.html.

Floyd, K. (2011). *Interpersonal Communication.* Boston: McGraw Hill.

Freeman, J.M. (1996). *Manners & Customs of the Bible.* New Kensington, PA.: Whitaker House.

Gibb, J.R. (1964). Climate for Trust Formation: T-Group Theory and Laboratory Methods. In Bradford, L.P. et al. Innovations in Re-Education (pp. 279 – 309) New York: Wiley.

Gibb, J.R. (1961). Defensive Communication. *Journal of Communication.* 141-148.

Gibson, J.W. & Hodgett, R.M. (1991). *Organizational Communication, A Managerial Perspective.* (2nd Ed.). New York: Harper Collins Publishers.

Graham, B. (1978). The Fruit of the Spirit. *The Holy Spirit.* Waco Texas: World Book Publishing. 180 – 211.

Guerrero, L.K., Anderson, P.S., & Walid, A. Communicating Closeness: Intimacy, Affection, and Social Support. In Stewart, J. (Ed.). *Bridges Not Walls.* 11th ed. New York: McGraw-Hill. Pp 275-289.

Gundry, P.H. (1981). *A Survey of The New Testament.* Grand Rapids, Michigan: Zondervan.

Harris, S. (2006). *Understanding The Bible.* New York: McGraw Hill.

Hurt, J. (2004). The Holy Spirit. Counseling through The Bible. (Vol. III). Dallas, Texas: Hope for the Heart. 1-20.

Halloman, H.W. (1994, Spring/Fall). The Relations of Christlikeness to Spiritual Growth. *Michigan theological Journal.* 57-85.

Hovland, C.I., Irving, J. L. & Kelly, H.H. (1965). *Communication and Persuasion.* New Haven: Yale University.

Jackson, B.S. (1972). A Descriptive Analysis of Four Vehicles of Communication in the Wayne County Department of Social Services' Communication Network. Unpublished Master's Essay. Wayne State University. Detroit, Michigan.

Jackson, B.S. (1981). A Correlational Analysis of the Relationship between the Attitude of Trust within a Communication Climate and Attitudes Toward Unions Among White-Collar Workers. Unpublished Doctoral Dissertation. Wayne State University, Detroit, Michigan.

Jackson, B.S. (2012). *CrossRoads.* Vol 1. The On-going Struggle. Detroit, Michigan: Priority ONE Publications.

Jensen, B.R. (2011). *More God, Less Crime.* Pennsylvania: Templeton Press.

Kelleman, R.W. (2004). The Art of Healing Spiritual Friendship. *Spiritual Friends: A Methodology of Soul Care and Spiritual Direction* (Vol II). Taneytown, MD: RPM Books. 147-214.

Lieth, N. (2011, October). Spiritual Rules for Our Lives. *Midnight Call.* 6-11.

Likert, R. (1967). *Human Organization.* New York: McGraw-Hill.

McMinn, M.D. (1996). Psychology, Theology, and Spirituality. *Christian Counseling.* Wheaton, Ill.: Tyndale House Publishers.

Mullinax, A.W. (1998). Biblical Cures that Counter Criminal Thinking. *Effective Jail & Prison Ministry for 21st Century.* USA: Coalition of Prison Evangelists Publications.

Newcomb, T.M. (1953). An Approach to the Study of Communicative Acts. *Psychological Review* 60. 149-150.

Parker, T. (1990). *Life After Life. Interviews with Twelve Murders.* London: Seches & Warburg.

Pierce, D.W. (2006). *Prison Ministry Hope Behind The Wall.* New York: The Haworth Pastoral Press.

Radmacher, E., Allen, R.B., and Huuse, H.W. (Eds.). (1999). *Nelson's New Illustrated Bible Commentary.* Nashville: Thomas Nelson.

Lebant, D.B. (2012). *Spiritual Freedom.* Retrieve July 27, 2012 from the World Wide Web: http://content.unity.org/prayer/inspirationalarticles/spiritualfreedom.html.

Richards, L.O. (1991). *The Bible Reader's Companion.* USA: HALO Press.

Richards, L.O. (1991). *New International Encyclopedia of Bible Words.* Grand Rapids, Michigan: Zondervan Publishing House.

Richards, L.O. (1987). *Teacher's Commentary.* USA: Victor Books.

Rogers, C.R. (1961). *On Becoming A Person.* Boston: Houghton Miffling Co.

Root, O. (1987). Life of Paul Part Two. *Training For Service, A Survey of The Bible.* Cincinnati, Ohio: Standard Publishing. 92-94.

Ryrie, C.C. (1972). *A Survey of Bible Doctrine.* Chicago: Moody Press.

Sachs, J. (2012). Turning Enemies into Friends. In Stewart, J. *Bridges Not Walls.* New York: McGraw Hill. 506-512.

Sanford, A.C., Hunt, G.T., & Bracey, H.J. (1976). *Communication Behavior in Organizations.* Ohio: Charles E. Merrill.

Sanford, C.C. & Bracey, H.J. (1972, October). Attitude Survey, A Tool for Improving Managerial Effectiveness. *Magazine of Bank Administrator.* 32-44.

Santos, M.G. (2006). *Inside Life Behind Bards in America.* New York: St. Martin' Press.

Sapsford, R.J. (1983). *Life Sentence Prisoners: Reacton, Response, And Change.* Open University Press.

Seay, T. (2002). *The Principles of Prison Ministry.* Xulan Press.

Tannenbaum, S. (1961). Carl R. Rogers and Non-Directive Teaching. In Rogers, C.R. *On Becoming A Person.* Boston: Haughton Mifflin.

Siang-Yang, T., & Clinton, T. (Speakers). (2012). Spiritual Direction, The Spiritual Disciplines and Christian Counseling. (CD Recording, Vol 18, Iss 4 American Association of Christian Counseling).

Siang-Yang, T. & Gregg, D.H. (1997). *Disciplines of The Holy Spirit.* Grand Rapids, Michigan: Zondervan.

Travis, L.F. (2008). *Introduction to Criminal Justice.* (6th ed.). Cincinnati, Ohio: Anderson Publishing.

Unger, M.T. & White, W. (Eds.). (1985). *Vines Complete Expository Dictionary of the Old and New Testament Words.* Nashville: Thomas Nelson Publishers.

Webb, E.J., Campbell, D.T., Schwartz, R.D. & Sechrest, L. (1972). Chicago: Rand McNally.

Wheeless, L.R. (1978, Winter). A Follow-up Study of the Relationship Among Trust, Disclosure and Interpersonal Solidarity. *Human Communication Research.* 4, 143.

Wheeless, L.R. & Gratz, J. (1976, Summer). Conceptualization and Measurement of Reported Self-Disclosures. *Human Communication Research.* 2, 238.

Whiston, W. (Translator). (1988). *The Works of Josephus, New Up Dated Edition.* Hendrickson Publishers.

Williams, J. (2000). *Sheep in Wolves Clothing, When the Actions of a Christian turn Criminal.* Chicago: Moody Press.

Wood, J.T. (2002). *Interpersonal Communication, Evryday Enco Nashville: Thomasunters.* (3rd ed.). USA: Thompson Learning, Inc.

Youngblood, R.F., Brace, F.F. & Harrison, R.K. (eds.). (1995). *Nelson's New Illustrated Bible Dictionary.* Nashville: Thomas Nelson.

ABOUT THE AUTHOR

Brenda Simuel Jackson (BA, MA, Master of Divinity, Ph.D. Certified Biblical Counselor), is a born again Christian, affiliated with the Baptist Denomination. She is a member and Minister of New Prospect Missionary Baptist Church, and does ministry through BSJ Christian Seminars, Inc., Prison/Jail Ministry. She is a graduate of Wayne State University, and Moody Theological Seminary – Michigan, formerly Michigan Theological Seminary. She is presently pursuing a second doctorate in Divinity at Jacksonville Theological Seminary with a concentration in prison ministry. She is a member of the pulpit, teaching, and prison ministries of her church.

Dr. Jackson has over thirty years of professional experience in human services, education administration, and management, as well as part-time collegiate instruction. She is currently a part-time faculty member of Wayne County Community College District. She has presented at Conferences of the American Association of Christian Counselors, local church women's retreats, mission programs, Christian Education Institutes, State Correctional Facilities, as well as Professional and Community Programs.

Dr. Jackson is a published writer who released her first book entitled, *A Journey of Redeeming Faith,* in April 2007. It was the first of four seminar compilations entitled, *Reflections on the Path to Wholeness.* The second in the series entitled, *Being Wonderfully Made"* was released April, 2008, and the third in the series, *Going Through",* was released in October, 2009. *Cross Roads,* the last in this series, was released in April, 2010. Another book entitled *Cross Roads,* is the first in the series, The Ongoing Struggle. This book is being released February, 2012. Dr.

Jackson also hosted a radio broadcast, "God's Teaching Moments." Her Christian Journey includes short term outreach mission and prison ministry assignments in Japan, South Africa, Jamaica, and Ghana. Dr. Jackson completed prison ministry in Zambia, Africa in December, 2011.

A native Detroiter, Dr. Jackson is a widow, a mother, grandmother, great grandmother, and ninth child of Willie and Lucy Simuel (both deceased). Dr. Jackson is a called minister of the Gospel. Dr. Jackson was licensed as a minister of the Gospel November 13, 2005. Having obtained a certification as a Chaplain; in 2013 Dr. Jackson obtained a Doctor of Philosophy in Divinity Degree with a major in prison ministry. Her vineyard is the prisons of the world.

BOOK ORDER FORM

The Ongoing Struggle: Vol 2
Freedom in a Cage
Brenda S. Jackson, Ph.D.

Name _____

Address _____

City _____ State _____ Zip _____

Phone _____ Fax _____

Email _____

Quantity	
Price *(each)*	$11.99
Subtotal	
S & H *(each)*	$1.99
MI Tax 6%	
TOTAL	

METHOD OF PAYMENT:
☐ Check or Money Order (*Make payable to*: BSJ Christian Seminars)

☐ Visa   ☐ Master Card   ☐ American Express
Acct No. _____ CVV _____

Expiration Date (*mmyy*) _____

Signature _____

Mail your payment with this form to:
BSJ Christian Seminars
P. O. Box 21004
Detroit, MI 48221
(313) 550-0081

BOOK ORDER FORM

The Ongoing Struggle: Vol 1
Cross Roads
Brenda S. Jackson, Ph.D.

Name _____

Address _____

City _____ **State** _____ **Zip** _____

Phone _____ **Fax** _____

Email _____

Quantity	
Price *(each)*	$11.99
Subtotal	
S & H *(each)*	$1.99
MI Tax 6%	
TOTAL	

METHOD OF PAYMENT:
❏ Check or Money Order (***Make payable to***: **BSJ Christian Seminars**)

❏ Visa   ❏ Master Card   ❏ American Express

Acct No. _____ CVV _____

Expiration Date (*mmyy*) _____

Signature _____

Mail your payment with this form to:
BSJ Christian Seminars
P. O. Box 21004
Detroit, MI 48221
(313) 550-0081

BOOK ORDER FORM

Reflections on the Path to Wholeness: Vol 1
A Journey of Redeeming Faith
Brenda S. Jackson, Ph.D.

Name _____

Address _____

City _____ State _____ Zip _____

Phone _____ Fax _____

Email _____

Quantity	
Price *(each)*	$9.99
Subtotal	
S & H *(each)*	$1.99
MI Tax 6%	
TOTAL	

METHOD OF PAYMENT:
☐ Check or Money Order (*Make payable to*: **BSJ Christian Seminars**)

☐ Visa ☐ Master Card ☐ American Express
Acct No. _____ CVV _____

Expiration Date (*mmyy*) _____

Signature _____

Mail your payment with this form to:
BSJ Christian Seminars
P. O. Box 21004
Detroit, MI 48221
(313) 550-0081

BOOK ORDER FORM

Reflections on the Path to Wholeness: Vol 2
Being Wonderfully Made
By Brenda S. Jackson, Ph.D.

Name _____

Address _____

City _____ **State** _____ **Zip** _____

Phone _____ **Fax** _____

Email _____

Quantity	
Price *(each)*	$11.99
Subtotal	
S & H *(each)*	$1.99
MI Tax 6%	
TOTAL	

METHOD OF PAYMENT:
☐ Check or Money Order (*Make payable to*: **BSJ Christian Seminars**)

☐ Visa ☐ Master Card ☐ American Express
Acct No. _____ CVV _____

Expiration Date (*mmyy*) _____

Signature _____

Mail your payment with this form to:
BSJ Christian Seminars
P. O. Box 21004
Detroit, MI 48221
(313) 550-0081

BOOK ORDER FORM

Reflections on the Path to Wholeness: Vol 3
Going Through
By Brenda S. Jackson, Ph.D.

Name _____
Address _____
City _____ **State** _____ **Zip** _____
Phone _____ **Fax** _____
Email _____

Quantity	
Price *(each)*	$11.99
Subtotal	
S & H *(each)*	$1.99
MI Tax 6%	
TOTAL	

METHOD OF PAYMENT:
❏ Check or Money Order (*Make payable to*: BSJ Christian Seminars)

❏ Visa ❏ Master Card ❏ American Express
Acct No. _____ CVV _____

Expiration Date (*mmyy*) _____

Signature _____

Mail your payment with this form to:
BSJ Christian Seminars
P. O. Box 21004
Detroit, MI 48221
(313) 550-0081

BOOK ORDER FORM

Reflections on the Path to Wholeness: Vol 4
Crossroads
Brenda S. Jackson, Ph.D.

Name _____

Address _____

City _____ **State** _____ **Zip** _____

Phone _____ **Fax** _____

Email _____

Quantity	
Price *(each)*	$11.99
Subtotal	
S & H *(each)*	$1.99
MI Tax 6%	
TOTAL	

METHOD OF PAYMENT:
❏ Check or Money Order (*Make payable to*: **BSJ Christian Seminars**)

❏ Visa   ❏ Master Card   ❏ American Express
Acct No. _____ CVV _____

Expiration Date (*mmyy*) _____

Signature _____

Mail your payment with this form to:
BSJ Christian Seminars
P. O. Box 21004
Detroit, MI 48221
(313) 550-0081

www.ingramcontent.com/pod-product-compliance
Lightning Source LLC
Chambersburg PA
CBHW052108070526
44584CB00017B/2393